Formation of Educational System in Uzbekistan

By:
Sirojiddinova Ugiloy

© Taemeer Publications LLC
Formation of Educational System in Uzbekistan
by: Sirojiddinova Ugiloy
Edition: August '2023
Publisher:
Taemeer Publications LLC (Michigan, USA / Hyderabad, India)

ISBN 978-93-5872-125-6

© Taemeer Publications

Book   :   *Formation of Educational System in Uzbekistan*
Author   :   Sirojiddinova Ugiloy

Publisher   :   Taemeer Publications
Year   :   '2023
Pages   :   32
Title Design :   *Taemeer Web Design*

MUSA TASHMUHAMMAD UGLI OYBEK

Annotation: In this article, the work of Musa Tashmuhammad son Oybek

Key words: Oybek, poetry, lyrics, nature, Kazoqboy Yoldoshev.

Oybek, the son of Musa Tashmuhammad, made a great contribution not only to Uzbek literature, but also to the literature of neighboring nations with his prolific work. even though his works consisted of simple poems devoted to the transient themes of the time, later Oybek began to express the most beautiful inner experiences of a person with lyrical feeling and sincerity. brought elegant lyricism to his work. Acquainted with the literature of the world and neighboring nations, under the influence of Uzbek classical literature, the poet's lyrical creativity improved. The well-known literary scholar Naim Karimov describes the rise of the poet's creativity as follows:"In this way, with the expansion of the scope of literary knowledge, Oybek's poetry was polished, enriched with new forms, colors and tones, and became beautiful like a fourteen-day moon".[2]

In the 1930s, Oybek published his series "Chimyon's notebook". Through this series, the poet showed that he turned lyric poetry into the mainstay of his work. It was through this series that the image of nature rose to the leading positions in Oybek's work. we can

On my head, the fragrant white flower of the apple,

I lie awake hugging the great earth.

If my ears are not enough, my heart is not enough,

The sun is kinder to a person's heart.[1]

The famous writer Mutriby Samarkandi in his work "Tazkirat ush-shuaro": "The dictionary meaning of the word "Poetry" is "to find and know". In this sense, the poet is called "the knower and the finder". sara finds words and gives their system a form that others cannot convey". while swimming in the ocean, he makes a pillow for himself from the "fragrant white flower of the apple". His lover does not reach something. However, the lyrical hero is calm. Because he knows that his heart can reach where the lover does not. it seems Only a poet can express such a lyrical image.

They say that a poem is a starfish.
No one can say that Bolchik lights the way.
A pearl is a thread of light in the darkness of life.
They say that poetry is only the language of birds
Sensitive souls crave meaning,
Or it is a teardrop of a blind soul,
Flowers on the stones.
They say that poetry is its own logic
Soft sleep comes from dreams,
The smell of the land that gave blood and joy
He didn't ask for inspiration with empty pride...[1]

In this poem, the poet expresses his thoughts in the image of nature. He compares the poem to the eyelash of a star, the tongue of a bird, the teardrop of a blind soul. The poem is an eyelash of a star. But no one can tell him "Bolchik light the way". Even if the poem is a "bird's language", it is such a language that only "sensitive souls" can understand it. Stones or flowers enjoy the "teardrop of a blind soul". "They say that poetry is its own logicsoft sleep" takes from the dream. However, "the smell of the land that gave blood and joy" inspirations cannot proudly ask.

There is more color on the horizons, more blood than that,

A caravan of clouds is hanging over my head.

He took my heart, I'm looking for it

Faithfulness is as good as truth.[1]

A poet is not an ordinary person. He can never be an ordinary person. Musa Tashmuhammad's son Aibek was one of those "different" people. As Aibek travels around the world, the "caravan of clouds" seems like a trap to him. " is looking for loyalty.

Let's pay attention to the last verses of this poem.

Like the moon rising, I'm crazy with love

Morning and an empty hut wait at my door.[1]

The poet remains true to his style even in the last stanzas of the poem. He compares the moon to a barkash and says that he is mad with love. The famous literary scholar, scientist, critic Kazoqboy Yoldoshev defines Oibek's love for nature as follows: "Oibek must have passed away as a more humane person who naturally sought solitude. Because only such a person can be happy with nature" and stops at one of his poetic lines.
Water was running down my face
Like a sad orphan girl.
The likening of the calm flowing clear water to a girl who cannot look directly into the eyes of a person, without an arrow, has never been in the experience of poetry. Usually, the girl's

lusciousness and the clarity of her face were compared to water. But the likening of water to a girl created the most appropriate, true and moving poetic scene in this place" [8].

In conclusion, I can say that Oibek's poetry is able to enchant any "whimsical" reader with its elegance and closeness to the heart. The subtle feelings of the inner world of a person are expressed through one or another phenomenon of nature. This style of expression gives naturalness to poetic verses.

REFERENCES:

1. Zarifa Saidnosirova. "My moon is mine." "New edition". Tashkent, 2019.

2. Karimov N. Buds made in Oybek Gulshan, T., 1985.
3. Yakubov H. The skill of the writer. Tashkent, Ozadabiynashar, 1966.
4. Koshjanov M. Oybek skills. Tashkent, Ozadabiynashar, 1965.
5. Karimov N. Oybek. Tashkent. G. Ghulam Publishing House of Literature and Art, 1985.
6. 6. Saidnosirova Z. Oybegim is mine. T.: East, 1994.

7. Ulug'ov A. Theory of literary studies. G. Ghulam Literature and Art Publishing House, Tashkent, 2018.

8. Kazakhboy Yoldoshev. Hot word. Generation of the new age. Tashkent, 2006.

Quality of education - New it is an important factor for the further development of Uzbekistan

Abstract: In this article O'The education system in the Republic of Uzbekistan, ongoing work on improving the quality of education, news, New O'The attention paid to education in Uzbekistan was discussed.

The key is so'z: New Uzbekistan, education system, "National Personnel Training Program", quality of education, o'teacher

As much as education is necessary for a person to reach adulthood and grow into a well-rounded person, education is equally important. Mankind was created with a sense instilled in him by God Almighty. It is the sense of knowing, and from birth to death man strives to know what he does not know and to teach others what he knows. The role and importance of education in the life of society is very great. The stronger, educated, potential people the society is, the more the state will develop and progress. We all know that every country that has set great goals and wants to achieve a high development position should first of all pay attention to the field of education. Including, focusing on education in the Republic of Uzbekistan - focusing on the future, preparation of the ground for high achievements is considered as one of the main ways for comprehensive development. If we look at the way Uzbekistan has traveled during the past period, our attention is drawn, first of all, to the work done to ensure people's well-being and economic stability. At the same time, we witness that special importance is given to the development of the educational system in these processes. As a proof of our word, we can say that Uzbekistan was the first among the CIS countries to develop the "National Personnel Training Program" in 1997, which envisages the gradual reform of the entire system of education. Even so, it is not a lie that there are some shortcomings in the education system of Uzbekistan. For many years, the discrimination of the teaching profession by the society, the lack of protection of its honor and dignity, the fact that students go to study only for the sake of obligation, unqualified teachers and educators, excessive red tape in the education system among them. First of all, when we talk about the education system, the image of the teacher comes to mind. How high the quality of education is, the growth of students' learning potential, the effective organization of lessons, of course, depends on the level of knowledge and talent of the teacher. Some of the situations we are observing in social networks are saddening. In one of them, the teacher is beaten by his student. and in another case, the parents insult the teacher. The President of the Republic of Uzbekistan, Shavkat Mirziyoyev, spoke about the personality of the teacher: "We are the representatives of the enlightened people who consider the teacher as great as a father and always honor him. When I think of a teacher, I imagine the dearest and most respected, intelligent and modern, sincere and kind people. Because this teacher gave lessons and education to all of us and raised us among our loving parents. Today, we are creating the foundations of a new era of development of Uzbekistan. In this, our closest assistants are teachers and trainers, scientific and creative intellectuals. Currently, a lot of practical work is being done to improve the quality of education. Eliminating the factors affecting the quality of education was identified as one of the main tasks. The establishment of the "Educational Quality Control Department" to improve the quality of the education system in our republic, to support every field of education, and to reveal shortcomings is one of the great steps to improve the quality of education. It's done. This department conducts its activities in accordance with the Constitution of the Republic of

Uzbekistan, the Law of the Republic of Uzbekistan "On Education", the National Program of Personnel Training, the decisions of the Chambers of the Oliy Majlis of the Republic of Uzbekistan, the President of the Republic of Uzbekistan decrees, decisions, orders, decisions and orders of the Cabinet of Ministers of the Republic of Uzbekistan, orders and legal instructions of the State Inspection and rectors of the institute, also conducts in accordance with the Regulations of the Department. It is commendable that the "Educational Quality Control Department" has done a number of effective works to improve the quality of education in the development of the educational system of Uzbekistan. But not all problems will be solved by the activity of this Department alone. Therefore, Uzbekistan has chosen the path of step-by-step reform in order to comprehensively develop its education system. It is not for nothing that the implemented reforms start from the field of pre-school education and upbringing. At the same time, when the attack of various foreign ideas increased sharply, it showed that the preschool education system, which is considered the most important link in the education of our children, is in an important place not only for the future of our society, but also for the future of our country. At this point, let me once again touch upon the teaching profession. We all know that until recent years, these professions have been attracted to work that they do not deserve. Among these are cotton picking and various cleaning jobs. But in recent years, the attitude towards the teaching profession has changed radically. We can see this in the increase of monthly salaries of teachers, in the positive change of people's attitude towards the owners of this profession. If the future of Uzbekistan is in the hands of competent young people, the role of mentors in the level of knowledge and potential of these young people and their development into mature personnel is incomparable. We are all aware of the

Referendum, which is expected to be held on April 30, in order to change and make additions to the Constitution of the Republic of Uzbekistan. One of the changes being made to this Constitution caught my attention. "In the Republic of Uzbekistan, the teacher's work is recognized as the basis for the development of society and the state, the formation and upbringing of a healthy, mature generation, the preservation and enrichment of the nation's spiritual and cultural potential.

    The state takes care of protecting the honor and dignity of teachers, their social and material well-being, and their professional growth" (Article 52). New Uzbekistan has chosen the right path of its development and is rapidly moving along this path. Today, our country is being recognized on world forums with its achievements, land and ground resources, good investment environment. Uzbekistan, which is working hard to rise, is drawing the right conclusions from the mistakes of other countries. A number of countries, which were among the developed and rich countries of the world in their time, are now in political, economic and cultural decline. The political scientists who analyzed the reasons for this, namely, the fact that the education system occupies a small place in the life of these countries, they think that attention to the education sector is lower than other sectors. Aware of this, Uzbekistan is working to make the educational system equal to the educational system of the most developed countries, and to provide it with the latest techniques and technologies. What can the quality of education give us? First of all, quality education is the main foundation for the future. Students who have received quality education will become mature staff. These personnel are not limited to their field, but can analyze other fields as well. Existing mistakes, shortcomings, advances progress. Such personnel serve earnestly for the development of the Motherland. And they themselves will try to prepare staff with mature potential like themselves in the future. Aware of this, Uzbekistan is working to make the educational system equal to the educational system of the most developed countries, and to provide it with the latest techniques and technologies. What can the quality of education give us? First of all, quality education is the main foundation for the future. Students who have received quality education will become mature staff. These personnel are not limited to their field, but can analyze other fields as well. Existing mistakes, shortcomings, advances progress. Such personnel serve earnestly for the development of the Motherland. And they themselves will try to prepare staff with mature potential like themselves in the future. Aware of this, Uzbekistan is working to make the educational system equal to the educational system of the most developed countries, and to provide it with the latest techniques and technologies. What can the quality of education give us? First of all, quality education is the main foundation for the future. Students who have received quality education will become mature staff. These personnel are not limited to their field, but can analyze other fields as well. Existing mistakes, shortcomings, advances progress. Such personnel serve earnestly for the development of the Motherland. And they themselves will try to prepare staff with mature potential like themselves in the future. is working to be provided with the latest techniques and technologies. What can the quality of education give us? First of all, quality education is the main foundation for the future. Students who have received quality education will become mature staff. These personnel are not limited to their field, but can analyze other fields as well. Existing mistakes, shortcomings, advances progress. Such personnel serve earnestly for the development of the Motherland. And they themselves will try to prepare staff with mature potential like themselves in the future. is working to be provided with the latest techniques and technologies. What can the quality of education give us? First of all, quality education is the main foundation for the future. Students who have received quality education will become mature staff. These personnel are not limited to their field, but can analyze other fields as well. Existing mistakes, shortcomings, advances progress. Such personnel serve earnestly for the development of the Motherland. And they themselves will try to prepare staff with mature potential like themselves in the future. they can analyze other fields as well. Existing mistakes, shortcomings, advances progress. Such personnel serve earnestly for the development of the Motherland. And they themselves will try to prepare staff with mature potential like themselves in the future. they can analyze other fields as well. Existing mistakes, shortcomings, advances progress. Such personnel serve earnestly for the development of the Motherland. And they themselves will try to prepare staff with mature potential like themselves in the future.

In conclusion, I can say that today the problem of the quality of education is one of the most urgent problems. We are all aware of the work being done to improve the quality of education and to eliminate deficiencies in the system. But let's not be satisfied with awareness alone. Let us contribute to the improvement of the quality of education and the creation of innovations in the field. How do you say? Let's instill in our children that the teaching profession is an honorable profession, let's introduce kindergartens, schools and universities as their second home, let's teach that physically and mentally mature young people are considered the future of the country. After all, New Uzbekistan is rich with young people who are aiming for new high goals.

REFERENCES

1. Bakhtiyor Kayumov. Quality education is the guarantee of our progress. Article. 2023.
2. yuz.uz
3. daryo.uz
4. m.aniq.uz

ILLUMINATION OF THE PROBLEMS OF THE PERIOD IN THE WORKS OF FREEDOM

Abstract: This article describes the characters of the stories, short stories and novels of Erkin A'zam, and comments on the adaptation of the characters to the era and their views and status.

Keyword: novel, short story, story, novel, period problem

When we get to know the novels, short stories and stories of the famous writer Erkin Azam, we can see that he has a unique, unique style. Folk phrases, sarcastic jokes are an integral part of the writer's works. The heroes of Erkin Azam are not indifferent to the times. The character of the characters is somewhat sharp and determined. As the literary critic Abdulla Ulug'ov admitted, "Erkin Azamov does not limit himself to the beautiful narration of the events and the impressive speech of the heroes. He strives to reveal the essence of events, to analyze the changes in the worldview of today's people" [5]. Erkin A'zam does not look far for his heroes. The people among the people, who know the people's pain, who served the people (Bolta Mardon. "Suv yakalab"), the characters whose life position is truth, truthfulness (Askar. The story "The year of his father's birth") make unpleasant evils in the life of the society. - realists who describe the truth and criticize them ruthlessly (Farhod Ramazon. The novel "Shovkin") and others are the main characters of his works.

In the works of Erkin A'zam, a number of problems of the era were also written. Farhod Ramazan, the main character in the novel "Shovqin" said, "Everybody speaks Uzbek, it's been a year or so since Uzbekistan became Uzbekistan, and they still don't remember those "second mother tongues". When dubbing the movie, they sing in Uzbek, and when they talk to each other, this is the situation!" through his words, we can witness that the writer wants to reveal many problems of the time through the work written about the people of cinema. While reading the work, our attention is drawn to Farhod Ramazan's opposition to the destruction of our language, nation, and national genes, as well as his hatred of vices that are taking root in society's life, such as greed and ambition.

The fact that he did not regret his actions even after leaving prison is not an unfamiliar situation for us. The hero of Erkin A'zam takes a critical approach to problems in the life of the society as an example of Ramadan. The character, feelings, and goals of contemporary people are revealed to some extent in this story. At the end of the story, mentioning the image of "Efendi" and comparing this image to the main character of the story, Ramazan, informs that there are still people like Efendi among our people who sing for the nation and teach us about humanity when the time comes.

Erkin Azam does not use beautiful similes in his works. The writer is not interested in the finer points of the samples of the artistic image. In each of his works, he tries to show some painful problem in the life of the society. He hides his purpose behind secret criticisms and sarcastic remarks. We can clearly see this in a number of the writer's works, including the novel "Noise", "Father's Birthday", "Lonely Boat", "Uncle", "Anoyi's Jaidari Apple", "Taziya". Erkin Azam has always tried to stay true to his style. Along the way, he gets acquainted with the creative world of different writers and learns from them. But he does not want to imitate anyone. The writer himself says about this: "I didn't know if it was close to my style or not, Aziz Nesin, I find the works of Fazil Iskandar, Vasiliy Aksyonov, Grant Matevosyan, Murad Muhammad Dost interesting. I may have learned something from them, but I have not tried to be like any of them. As much as we can, we are going to be a blessing, who knows" [4].

In conclusion, I can say that Erkin Azam made a significant contribution to modern Uzbek literature with his works. The writer proved to be a creative person with his own words and style. We can witness that Erkin A'zam's pen is a sharp writer from the fact that some of the problems of the time that he revealed are still relevant today.

REFERENCES
1. Free Member. The water is boiling. Heaven itself is the rule. - T.: "Sharq", 2007.
2. Free Member. Otoyi's birthday. - T.: "Gafur Ghulam", 1981.
3. Free Member. Noise. "Uzbekistan" T.: 2001.
4. www.ziyo.uz.com
5. kh-davron.uz

OUR INITIATIVE, TALENT, POWER - FOR THE MOTHERLAND

Abstract: This article reflects on the love, service and preservation of the country and the events that have taken place in this regard today and in the past.

Keyword: "On state policy regarding youth", national anthem, boxing, Turon, Turkestan, Movarounnahr.

We humans have been blessed with unlimited blessings by God Almighty. The greatest of these is our homeland. It is our happiness to be born in the so-called paradise country of Uzbekistan. I heard a legend when I was a child. It says that Allah Almighty is the land for His servantsHe divided different parts of his face to make the Motherland. For us Uzbeks, he has reserved a place in a piece of heaven. I don't know how true this myth is, but I believe that Uzbekistan is a heavenly country. The name of our heavenly country, which was called Turan, Turkestan, Mavorunnahr in ancient times, connected the East and the West through the Great Silk Road, and cultivated thousands of alloma and fuzlao in its bosom, is being proudly mentioned in the pulpits of the world today. Our country, which is considered to be a part of heaven, surprises the world with its beauty. Today, Uzbekistan has taken a place among the politically, economically, and culturally developed countries on a world scale. The impact of the changes, news, and development taking place in our country today affects every region, district, I am not mistaken when I say that it is manifested in the village. All these changes are for our people to live peacefully, live a free life, and take bold steps for the future. After all, the prayers and hardships of our hardworking people have a great role in today's achievements.

Above, we talked about the conditions created for our people to live comfortably. The wide range of opportunities created for our youth is especially noteworthy. Implementation of the educational standards of the developed countries of the world in Uzbekistan, educational cooperation with countries such as Finland, Japan, Germany, conditions created for practicing all kinds of sports, mechanics, chemistry, all the ways opened for conducting research in the fields are all for us young people to grow up as mature people, to develop as individuals with their own worldview. At this point, the question arises. Yes, so many opportunities are being created for our youth in our country, but are we young people taking advantage of them and realizing their value? that's right There are many of us who raised the flag of the country and made its name known. The achievements of our athletes, young chess players, the results of our young scientists who won prestigious world competitions in mathematics and chemistry, and many other victories are worthy of praise. The results achieved by our young athletes Gulsevar Ganiyeva (boxing), Sharifa Davronova (athletics), the youngest Paralympian of 2022 Azizbek Boynazarov (para swimming), and our young chess players Javahir Sindorov, Nodirbek Yaqubboyev, Jahangir Vahidov and others are pleasing to all of us today. I'm not wrong if I say that he raised like a mountain. But we must not stop there. The current era demands from us young people to search and act. The further development of our country, In order to be able to easily compete with any developed country in the world, we, the youth, have a great place. Let's not talk about the homeland. Let's contribute to its comprehensive development. Perhaps, this action of ours will not bear fruit in fifteen years, but one day, when we see our young people who are sincerely working for the Motherland in every field of our country, bravely guarding the country's borders, our hearts will surely be like a stone. will rise.

  The fast-paced life is preparing new tasks and tests for people every day. At the same time, we are making unexpected gifts for people. It's not a secret to all of us that as the pace of life accelerates, people's hearts lose feelings of love, compassion, and sincerity. We are witnessing the fact that our youth, who imitated the West and are interested in their easy life, have moved away from our national mentality, their language and culture. Even the feeling of love for the country is seen as something insignificant in the eyes of many young people. Let's analyze how true this is. We take it for granted when a kid on the street loudly sings a hit song. But if the anthem or songs about the Motherland are played, please lower the volume. What our great ancestors did, we will talk about the discoveries they made, works that surprised the world. We say that Alisher Navoi wrote the famous work "Khamsa", and most of us have not memorized ten verses of that work. In my opinion, children should be raised in the spirit of love for the country and loyalty to the people from a young age. The Japanese have such a tradition. from childhood, they try to raise them in the spirit of love and loyalty to their country and people. Treason is considered the greatest sin for them. We should also raise our children from childhood in the spirit of patriotism, loyalty to the nation, and respect for the pure name of our ancestors. it is necessary to start a number of effective activities in pre-school educational institutions, schools, and higher education institutions. if their children are asked about our country, flag, coat of arms and anthem, if they are taught what they don't know, it will serve as a good foundation for the future generation. If our children sing our national anthem with joy, sing poems about Uzbekistan and the Uzbek people, if they grow up realizing that serving the Motherland is the highest happiness, no evil force will be able to attack our beloved country Uzbekistan. It is up to us how to educate the owners of tomorrow. Let's not be careless in this matter! no evil force can attack our beloved country Uzbekistan. It is up to us how to educate the owners of tomorrow. Let's not be careless in this matter! no evil force can attack our beloved country Uzbekistan. It is up to us how to educate the owners of tomorrow. Let's not be careless in this matter!

We are all aware of the five important initiatives of the President of the Republic of Uzbekistan to raise the morale of young people and meaningfully organize their free time. I am not mistaken in saying that these initiatives have shown their results in a short time. The first initiative was aimed at increasing the interest of young people in music, painting, literature, theater and other types of art. They say, "No evil comes from a person who loves art." It is precisely these beautiful songs created by our artists, several masterpieces written by our writers, that reach even the remotest regions of the world today and inform about Uzbekistan. Our people are benefiting from their works created in the spirit of patriotism, and our youth are growing up with this feeling. The second initiative: Physical training of young people, aimed at creating the necessary conditions for them to demonstrate their abilities in the field of sports. We are all aware of the great victories achieved by our athletes. We are witnessing that nothing can introduce a country to the world as quickly as sports. It is these athletes who raise the flag of our country in the world arenas. The third initiative: aimed at organizing the effective use of computer technologies and the Internet among the population and young people. Now is the age of internet technology. Of course, it is good to use modern technologies, to be aware of various electrical equipment. But at the same time, we should not forget that various foreign ideas and attacks against our national ideology are entering through these Internet technologies. our people, The role of this initiative is very important to protect our youth, who are the foundation of our future, from such pressures. A person whose mind is filled with foreign ideas and ideologies will never be able to serve the country. His strength and intelligence are used by evil people who do not see the peace of our free land. The fourth initiative: aimed at organizing systematic work on raising the morale of young people, widely promoting reading among them. A spiritual person will never betray the country. No evil force can take advantage of such a person. In our country, a number of effective activities are underway to bring up such spiritual, cultured, patriotic people. Promotion of reading among the population is one of them. The book is the grower of the human mind, is the main source that enriches his worldview. If our youth is aware of the heroism of Jalaluddin Manguberdi, Temur Malik, and Amir Temur from childhood, if they grow up under the influence of the works of Alisher Navoi, Zahiruddin Muhammad Babur, if they memorize hadiths from the books of Imam Bukhari and Imam Termizi, then no evil can defeat a country with such generations. The future of our independent Uzbekistan will be even greater. The fifth initiative: deals with women's employment issues. We know that the biggest influence on a child is its mother. If a mother has a broad mind and a healthy worldview, this will not fail to affect her child as well. If our mothers do not go out, if they do not know what changes and innovations are happening in the society, how will they educate the owners of our future. At a glance, These five initiatives may seem to be for our people and our youth. After all, at the core of these five initiatives, another development path of our heavenly country is reflected.

As we all know, "Uzbekistan" publishing house has published a collection called "Activity Chronicle of the President of the Republic of Uzbekistan Shavkat Mirziyoyev". In it, the chronicle of the political activity of the head of our state from September 2016 to January 1, 2020 is reflected in detail. It is known that this period - with the names "New

Uzbekistan", "New stage of Uzbekistan's development" occupies a very important place in the history of our country and in the series of our relations with the world community. This period is the period that completely changed Uzbekistan, the political, social and economic relations in the life of our society, introduced our country to the whole world in a new, democratic image. This period played a big role in the life of our youth. Young people of new Uzbekistan showed themselves in every field. After that, let's work together under the leadership of our President for the formation of a new image of independent Uzbekistan. Educated young people are needed to build a new Uzbekistan. They should serve as shoulder mates for the further development of Uzbekistan. Let's join forces for this work. If we do not act and fight for our country, no one will come, develop and protect it. Everything is in the hands of our youth.

New Uzbekistan is speeding towards new goals. I am not mistaken in saying that the new opportunities created by the new Uzbekistan for young people were the lifelong dream of us young people. According to the Law of the Republic of Uzbekistan "On State Policy Regarding Youth" adopted in 2016, the state policy regarding youth serves to create conditions for social formation of young people and development of their intellectual, creative and other potential. New Uzbekistan's new development path is different than ever. It is necessary for us young people to act so that there are no obstacles on this path.There is a saying among our people that "service to others is the highest duty". We know this sentence well, but we do not fully understand its meaning. Because many people who hear this sentence think of military personnel and their service to the Motherland. I do not mean to say that they do not serve the country. Every person who was born in this country, grew up in this country, regardless of nationality, should serve this country. It is not necessary to be a military officer or work in a government office for this great service. Every person who truly loves his country, people, and family should have his heart beating for his country. At this point, the question arises as to how we can serve the Motherland. For example, I am an ordinary student. I have a great task ahead of our country in the future. That is, I teach young people who are considered the future of the country. It is my honor to educate hundreds and thousands of young people who serve the country. As a teacher, it has become one of my biggest dreams to see the growth of my students, to see them serving the Motherland wholeheartedly. I have to work tirelessly on this path. This is the biggest task not only for me, but for all teachers and coaches. At this point, let's remember the Pandemic period. Due to the efforts of our passionate doctors, the lives of many of our patients have been saved. They mobilized all their forces to fight against the disease. With this, they proved that they are true children of our country. They are still valiantly fighting this disease. Not only teachers or doctors, the nation of our country, If all citizens, regardless of their job and profession, spend all their efforts on the development of this country, if they try so that it will not be left behind by any country, I think that a country with such a people will never stop developing. Let's not forget that we are a great force together. If we do not give all our love for this country, the evil forces who do not see the peace of our country will try to take it from us. Our people have always fought with all their might for the peace and freedom of our country. Thank goodness we live in peaceful and prosperous times. Let us not forget the blood shed for this peace. Let us serve the Motherland with all our talent and energy. This is the duty of every citizen to the Motherland. If all citizens, regardless of their profession, put all their efforts into the development of this country, if they try to ensure that it does not fall behind any country, I think that a country with such a people will never stop developing. Let's not forget that we are a great force together. If we do not give all our love for this country, the evil forces who do not see the peace of our country will try to take it from us. Our people have always fought with all their might for the peace and freedom of our country. Thank goodness we live in peaceful and prosperous times. Let us not forget the blood shed for this peace. Let us serve the Motherland with all our talent and energy. This is the duty of every citizen to the Motherland. If all citizens, regardless of their profession, put all their efforts into the development of this country, if they try to ensure that it does not fall behind any country, I think that a country with such a people will never stop developing. Let's not forget that we are a great force together. If we do not give all our love for this country, the evil forces who do not see the peace of our country will try to take it from us. Our people have always fought with all their might for the peace and freedom of our country. Thank goodness we live in peaceful and prosperous times. Let us not forget the blood shed for this peace. Let us serve the Motherland with all our talent and energy. This is the duty of every citizen to the Motherland. I think that a country with such people will never stop developing. Let's not forget that we are a great force together. If we do not give all our love for this country, the evil forces who do not see the peace of our country will try to take it from us. Our people have always fought with all their might for the peace and freedom of our country. Thank goodness we live in peaceful and prosperous times. Let us not forget the blood shed for this peace. Let us serve the Motherland with all our talent and energy. This is the duty of every citizen to the Motherland. I think that a country with such people will never stop developing. Let's not forget that we are a great force together. If we do not give all our love for this country, the evil forces who do not see the peace of our country will try to take it from us. Our people have always fought with all their might for the peace and freedom of our country. Thank goodness we live in peaceful and prosperous times. Let us not forget the blood shed for this peace. Let us serve the Motherland with all our talent and energy. This is the duty of every citizen to the Motherland. Our people have always fought with all their might for the peace and freedom of our homeland. Thank goodness we live in peaceful and prosperous times. Let us not forget the blood shed for this peace. Let us serve the Motherland with all our talent and energy. This is the duty of every citizen to the Motherland. Our people have always fought with all their might for the peace and freedom of our homeland. Thank goodness we live in peaceful and prosperous times. Let us not forget the blood shed for this peace. Let us serve the Motherland with all our talent and energy. This is the duty of every citizen to the Motherland.

In conclusion, I can say that no person who worked for his country and served it faithfully will be despised. If we have the talent, if we direct it for this country, for its development, if we do our best so that no evil will come to the threshold of this country, if we try to prevent any evil from entering our people, then we will take the initiative so that the name of our country will always be heard among the developed countries. If we pray, we will receive God's pleasure and the prayers of our people. There can be no greater happiness for a person than this. After all, the young generation growing up after us will take an example from us.

REFERENCES

1.isrs.uz
2.lex.uz
3.uz.m.wikipedia
4.kun.uz

ALL OPPORTUNITIES- FOR NATURE, TO PRESERVE NATURE

Allah Almighty has given us human beings great blessings for us to use and enjoy. The most valuable of these blessings is nature. Nature is the land of miracles created by Allah, the world of vegetation, which has a place for thousands of animals, plants and other living beings. In Nasiruddin Rabguzi's "Kissasi Rabguzi" it is written as follows: "Allah created the whole universe in six days." (Verse) "Badahqiq, We created the heavens, the earth and everything between them in six days". created, created the waters on Wednesday, called the winds, the clouds, collected the trees, the grass, shared the sustenance, heaven on Thursday, He created hell, the angels of mercy and torment, the angels, He created Adam on Friday, He did not create anything on Saturday. It had the power to create all things and thousands more in the blink of an eye. That is why he created in six days, in which there was a lesson for his servants: "I do not hurry even if I am able." The Messenger of God said: "Hurry is the work of Satan and not hastening is the work of the Most Merciful" [1]. So, man was created after the sun and stars, the animal and plant world. And by the command of Allah, he had all of them. Nature itself is like a skilled jeweler. Every plant, every tree, forest, river, animal world that sprouted from his bosom is a world of its own. The ability to live in such a world is one of the main achievements of us humans. But do we humans appreciate this achievement? Do we know the value of the wealth that nature has gifted us? Unfortunately, no. The World Meteorological Center, part of the United Nations, states: "Out of the 10 biggest disasters of the last 50 years, drought has the highest death toll (650,000 deaths)" [2]. Now let's think that a large part of the population of the Earth is dying because of the lack of water. And we are currently at the peak of water wastage. According to the conclusions of the Stockholm International Peace Research Institute, there are two main causes of global hunger: the first is climate change, and the second is armed conflict [3]. Let's focus on the first reason. The phenomenon of climate change is being observed on Earth from year to year. This process entered the list of global problems many years ago. A question arises here. What causes climate change? Why is this process accelerating year by year? The reason is that man, who is considered a supreme being, could not preserve the wealth given to him. Knowing nature as an "inexhaustible resource", he used it. He did not think that this "inexhaustible supply" would one day run out. Today, the whole Earth, including our Motherland, Uzbekistan, is struggling with many environmental problems. Today, Uzbekistan has become a large industrialized, agrarian zone. The development of our country, joining the ranks of the most advanced countries of the world, certainly pleases every citizen of Uzbekistan. But it is also appropriate to ensure the security of our national ecosystem in the path of development. There are a number of ecological problems in the Republic of Uzbekistan today, and without finding a solution to them, we cannot preserve our national ecology. They are:

1. Problems related to nature protection in Fergana, Navoi, Margilon, Chirchik, Angren, Almalyk and other areas of large industrialization. The socio-ecological situation in these regions is bad, and various gases and wastes coming out of industrial centers are causing environmental damage.

2. Environmental problems in the agro-industrial complex and their unsolved problems for many years.

3. Contamination of natural waters with waste from industrial centers, pesticides and mineral fertilizers.

4. Problems related to the protection and restoration of flora and fauna, expanding the network of nature reserves and national parks.

Consistent efforts are being made in our country to protect the environment, rational use of natural resources, improvement of sanitary and ecological conditions, and preservation of national ecology. One of them is the law of the President of the Republic of Uzbekistan dated October 30, 2019 "On approval of the concept of environmental protection of the Republic of Uzbekistan until 2030". This Concept includes:

- preservation and quality of environmental objects (atmospheric air, water, land, soil, subsoil, biodiversity, protected natural areas) from anthropogenic influence and other negative influencing factors;
- priority use of materials, products, production facilities and other facilities that pose the least ecological risk;
- expansion of protected natural areas;
- ensuring environmentally safe use of toxic chemicals and radioactive substances;
- improvement of the ecologically safe system of waste management;
- includes measures to form the ecological culture of the population, increase the level of transparency of the activities of state bodies in the field of environmental protection, and strengthen the role of civil society [4].

The adoption of such laws and decisions is certainly not without benefits. But protecting nature is not only the duty of the state or responsible persons. Every citizen of the Republic of Uzbekistan should protect the environment, environmental objects: land, water, soil, atmospheric air, etc., and ensure that they serve the future generations.

The famous scientist Yu.Odum says about environmental problems in nature: "Eliminating ecological problems, keeping the environment stable and safe, only the joint action of the world community and the legal regulation of these actions can bring humanity out of the ecological crisis." Planet Earth is the common home of mankind. Today, the total population of the earth is 6 billion. All 6 billion people use the natural resources of water, air, soil and other resources. Due to the negative attitude of mankind to nature, a number of pressing problems have arisen. Today, the implementation of economical, safe, environmentally friendly technologies in solving environmental problems, nature protection, Efforts to consistently carry out activities related to its conservation or to improve the legislation related to the sector show that the issued laws are not enough to solve them. Vigilance is the need of the times. The inhabitants of the entire Earth should not be indifferent to the environment and the ecological problems related to it, and should be alert to such urgent issues.

Our forefathers treasured every inch of our land and appreciated every drop of water. We young people were also brought up in the spirit of protecting nature. We should raise our children from childhood to protect nature and its resources, and to criticize the wastages happening around us.

In conclusion, I can say that we should not ignore the problems related to nature. Let one person plant a tree today. Let someone else make good use of water resources or prevent leaf burn in the fall season. Over time, the number of these individuals will reach a hundred, from a hundred to a thousand. In this way, all the inhabitants of the Earth get used to this way of life. Conservation of nature begins with the smallest actions. That is, simply turning off the water that flows in vain, and not throwing garbage on the streets is also a contribution to the preservation of nature.

REFERENCES
1. Nasiruddin Rabguzi. Narrated by Rabguzi.
2. www.kalampir.uz
3. www.zamon.uz
4. www.lex.uz

www.ingramcontent.com/pod-product-compliance
Lightning Source LLC
LaVergne TN
LVHW010422070526
838199LV00064B/5391